LITTLE BOOK OF

Australian
Gardens

GW00706104

NATIONAL LIBRARY OF AUSTRALIA

Canberra 2005

Published by the National Library of Australia
Canberra ACT 2600
Australia

Little book of Australian gardens.

ISBN 0 642 27631 5.

1. Historic gardens - Australia - Pictorial works.
2. Gardens in art. 3. Gardens - Poetry.
4. Australian poetry.
I. National Library of Australia.

A821.0080364

Compiled by Sarah Gleeson-White, with photography by Trisha Dixon
Designed by Kathryn Wright Design
Printed by Lamb Print

Front cover illustration:
Trisha Dixon (b.1953)
Stairway, Glen Rannoch, Mount Macedon, Victoria 1998
col. slide; 35 mm
Pictures Collection, National Library of Australia
nla.pic-an23098647

Back cover illustration:
Trisha Dixon (b.1953)
Rose Garden, Gidleigh, Bungendore, New South Wales 1999
col. slide; 35 mm
Pictures Collection, National Library of Australia
nla.pic-an23122747

Contents

❧ Australian Autumn ❧

DOROTHEA McKELLAR

This is the gentlest season of the year.
　　From mists of pearl and gold
　　The slow sweet hours unfold
　　To crystal colours, still
　　As a glass, but not so chill.

All birds speak softly in the autumn Bush.
　　One bellbird from the deep
　　Like a call heard in sleep
　　Chimes: in the bronze-gold gloom
　　Cool greenhood orchids bloom.

Brown leaves are withering on the alien trees:
　　The bronze green of our hills
　　Is veiled with blue that fills
　　The spirit with a bright
　　Sense of intrinsic light.

Now that the dew has vanished, sheep lie down
　　By companies content
　　In wilga-shade and scent;
　　The reaper sounds near by
　　Like the cicadas' cry.

And so the mellow day flows on to dusk
　　And loveliness that grows
　　From skies of mauve and rose,
　　While fragrant smoke-plumes lie
　　Subtle as memory.

Curled round our hearts in this still jewelled air,
    Risen from the pulsing fire
    Many-hued like desire.
    Overhead, stars blaze white,
    Superb in frosty night.

This is the kindliest season of the year.
    The sun's gold arrows all
    Have lost their barbs: thick fall
    The berries ripe, and still
    The birds may have their fill.

Now peace and plenteousness have spread their wings
    After the blessèd rains
    On Autumn's hills and plains.
    We too give thanks and bless
    This southland's graciousness.

(page 1)
Trisha Dixon (b.1953)
Bird Bath, Michelago Station, NSW 2001
Private Collection

❦ Dear Little Cottage ❦

JOHN SHAW NEILSON

'Tis not for the white lilies, white lilies and tall:
The grass has outlived them, it grows by the wall
    Of the dear little cottage that I know...

'Tis not for the cherries — the cherries are wild,
And into their branches has clambered no child
    To drink up the blood of a cherry.

'Tis not for the river, hemmed in by the weir,
Or the lilt of the winds in the glow of the year
    When the birds o' the water make merry...

A spell is upon me, and why should I stray
When I have fine company all the long day
    In the dear little cottage that I know.

It is for the voices, the voices that blessed,
The lips that made music, the hands that caressed
    In the dear little cottage that I know.

It is for the shadows that sit by the door,
The feet that go tripping the old broken floor
    At night when the fiddles are shrieking.

It is for the counsel, long-loving and wise,
The hopes that were born in a legion of sighs...
    The lips (oh, the cold lips) are speaking.

It is for a temple enshrouded in mist,
A rosy girl raising her face to be kissed
    In the dear little cottage that I know.

Trisha Dixon (b.1953)
Romani, Bendemeer, New South Wales [between 1990 and 1993]
col. transparency; 6.0 x 6.0 cm
Pictures Collection, nla.pic-an10716247-27

Trisha Dixon (b.1953)
Secret Garden, Pear Tree Cottage, Dunkeld, Victoria 2004
col. slide; 35 mm
Private Collection

❧ *Amongst the Roses* ❧

HENRY KENDALL

I walked through a Forest, beneath the hot noon,
On Etheline calling and calling!
One said: "She will hear you and come to you soon,
When the coolness, my brother, is falling."
But I whispered: "O Darling, I falter with pain!"
And the thirsty leaves rustled, and hissed for the rain,
Where a wayfarer halted and slept on the plain;
  And dreamt of a garden of Roses!
   Of a cool sweet place,
   And a nestling face
  In a dance and a dazzle of Roses.

In the drouth of a Desert, outwearied, I wept,
O Etheline, darkened with dolours!
But, folded in sunset, how long have you slept
By the Roses all reeling with colours?
A tree from its tresses a leaf did shake,
It fell on her face, and I feared she would wake,
So I brushed it away for *her* sweet sake;
  In that garden of beautiful Roses!
   In the dreamy perfumes
   From rich red blooms
  In a dance and a dazzle of Roses.

❧ *Déjeuner sur l'herbe* ❧

BRUCE BEAVER

Everywhere I look in the garden
I see old cutlery —
Old knives, forks, spoons,
Greened-over silver and worn down
Handles of bone.
It is as though my mother
Has made a meal of her gardening.
I knew she drew sustenance from it
But never quite equated the garden
With a banquet of multitudinous courses,
From escargots on the half shell
To crème de Carnation;
From mud pies to chives and chokos.
She has laid her table and spread upon it
A green cloth of couch.
Not quite a cordon bleu
Of a garden nor yet a cafeteria.
Uninvited guests abound:
The minute gluttonous sparrow;
The picking pernickety dove;
The gourmet peewit
And the gate-crashing cat
Who's all for gobbling guests.
Morning and noon she dines
Jabbing and spooning at half-baked soil.
Of an evening she stands and hoses
Drinking in the quenched garden.

Trisha Dixon (b.1953)
Herb Garden, Salisbury Court, Uralla, New South Wales 1999
col. slide; 35 mm
Pictures Collection, nla.pic-an23122566

At night in moon or star shine
Or no shine at all
I count the clicking glinting cutlery
Like a servant of the house
Making light of my task
In the knowledge of belonging.

❧ *Song of Murray's Brigade* ❧

BANJO PATERSON

Small birds singing in the tree tops tell
    Where runs the river of my home;
And the wistful wishing of the folk who love us well
    And follow us wherever we may roam.

And our hearts go back to the folk beside the river
    To the land where the sheep and cattle roam.
It's a long, long job, but we'll finish it together
    For every mile we travel leads us home.

No songs greet us for the birds are mute
    The aeroplane's the only thing to fly.
Upward to the pilot send a special brand salute
    For we may need him badly bye and bye.

Soldiers singing as their fancies come
    New songs, old songs, they sang another day.
Thus they sing and march to the beating of the drum
    Till orders come to put the drums away.

And our hearts go back to the folk beside the river
    To the land where the sheep and cattle roam.
It's a long, long job, but we'll finish it together
    For every mile we travel leads us home.

Trisha Dixon (b.1953)
Bolaro Station, Adaminaby,
New South Wales
col. transparency; 6.0 x 6.0 cm
Private Collection

❦ *Autumn Rain* ❦

GWEN HARWOOD

Chill rain: the end of autumn.
A day of sombre music,
a raindrop army drumming

to the plover's haunting cry.
Grief under a gold mask,
perhaps? More likely, joy

at the delicate abundance
stirring in sodden paddocks
to nourish generations

of spurred grey wings. A day
for the householder to listen
in peace to his tanks filling,

or watch the mushrooms making
themselves from almost nothing
in their chosen place, a domed

city among the pines;
but to any eye beneath them
dark suns with rays extending.

A day to think of death,
perhaps, or of children's children
inheriting the earth.

Trisha Dixon (b.1953)
Durrol, Mount Macedon, Victoria 1999
col. transparency; 6.0 x 6.0 cm
Pictures Collection, nla.pic-an23123717

❀ *Florobiography* ❀

CHRIS WALLACE-CRABBE

At first,
leaving aside the lairy purple of garage morning glories,
it was nasturtiums that spoke of colour
and I boldly chewed their leaves,
walking along the brick edge of a gardenbed,
to please a little girl called Jill.

Then it was bulbs
in a sandy springtime
bursting alight under the edge of apple-trees,
breaking the green with
the different characters of
jonquil, grape hyacinth and freesia.

Buddleia trumpets
dangled their flopping creamy-white
through my perfectly undistinguished
teenagerhood:
they were nothing special, except for the bees.

In the northern hemisphere
with its overstated seasons
I came in time to meet
the daffodil and crocus
of European literature,
treating them as if they were nightingales.

Pepper-and-salt years
of empirical observation
taught me to feather like a parrot
at all the teasing varieties
of hairy gum-tree blossom,
through summers of my discontent

with the universe itself,
loving the parts of it, though, little by little,
as the beak of an eastern spinebill goes into the hakea.

Trisha Dixon (b.1953)
Walled Garden in Clarendon, Tasmania
[between 1990 and 1993]
col. transparency ; 6.0 x 6.0 cm
Pictures Collection, nla.pic–an10716247–29

❧ *The Lark* ❧

LESLIE H. ALLEN

The air was hazed, and charged with blossom-scent,
A tingling white was in the firmament,
The drowsy noon lay on the yellow sheep
And bronzen oranges that basked in sleep.
The air was wrinkled o'er the heated grass,
Leaf shadows flecked the sand in the stream's glass—
I caught it in my fingers, and it spread
In golden sparkles like that song o'erhead.
Up went my eager vision, all afloat
To catch some light-line on the hidden throat
That drank the blue, and turned it into song.
Straight up above me, in the noon-rays strong,
There shot the upward throat, and as I stood
The spread wings burst into a shower of blood;
Then the sun-drunken Spirit was fled; there leapt
A magic where the bronzen fruitage slept.
The flame-strings of the blossom shook their blaze
Trembling and song filled all the heavy haze.

Trisha Dixon (b.1953)
Gidleigh, Bungendore, New South Wales 1999
col. slide; 35 mm
Pictures Collection, nla.pic-an23122580

❧ Flowering Eucalypt in Autumn ❧

LES MURRAY

That slim creek out of the sky
the dried-blood western gum tree
is all stir in its high reaches:

its strung haze-blue foliage is dancing
points down in breezy mobs, swapping
pace and place in an all-over sway

retarded en masse by crimson blossom.
Bees still at work up there tack
around their exploded furry likeness

and the lawn underneath's a napped rug
of eyelash drift, of blooms flared
like a sneeze in a redhaired nostril,

minute urns, pinch-sized rockets
knocked down by winds, by night-creaking
fig-squirting bats, or the daily

parrot gang with green pocketknife wings.
Bristling food for tough delicate
raucous life, each flower comes

as a spray in its own turned vase,
a taut starbust, honeyed model
of the tree's fragrance crisping in your head.

When the Japanese plum tree
was shedding in spring, we speculated
there among the drizzling petals

what kind of exquisitely precious
artistic bloom might be gendered
in a pure ethereal compost

of petals potted as they fell.
From unpetalled gum-debris
we know what is grown continually,

a tower of fabulous swish tatters,
a map hoisted upright, a crusted
riverbed with up-country show towns.

Trisha Dixon (b.1953)
Fulling Garden, Eltham, Victoria 1999
col. slide; 35 mm
Pictures Collection, nla.pic-an23098516

❧ *Morning Peace* ❧

ARTHUR H. ADAMS

The sudden sunbeams slant between the trees
Like solid bars of silver, moonlight kissed,
And strike the supine shadows where they rest
Stretched sleeping; while a timid, new-born Breeze
Stirs through the grasses, petulant — her eyes
Half-blinded by the clinging scarves of mist:
Her robes, that tangled through the grasses twist,
Weave as she moves sweet whispered melodies.

O, may it be morn like this, when slow
From a dark world beneath my soul shall go
Through the wet grasses of a purple plain,
Still stretching broader in the cool, grey glow
Of morning twilight: then my soul shall know
That life and love are lost — and found again!

Trisha Dixon (b.1953)
Kitchen Garden, Bobundara, Cooma, NSW 1997
col. transparency; 6.0 x 6.0 cm
Private Collection

Trisha Dixon (b.1953)
Hascombe Garden, Mount Macedon, Victoria 1997
col. slide; 35 mm
Pictures Collection, nla.pic-an23122230

A Mid-Summer Noon in the Australian Forest

CHARLES HARPUR

Not a sound disturbs the air,
There is quiet everywhere;
Over plains and over woods
What a mighty stillness broods!

All the birds and insects keep
Where the coolest shadows sleep;
Even the busy ants are found
Resting in their pebbled mound;
Even the locust clingeth now
Silent to the barky bough:
And over hills and over plains
Quiet, vast and slumbrous, reigns.

Only there's a drowsy humming
From yon warm lagoon slow coming:
'Tis the dragon-hornet—see!
All bedaubéd resplendently,
With yellow on a tawny ground—
Each rich spot nor square nor round,
Rudely heart-shaped, as it were
The blurred and hasty impress there,
Of a vermeil-crusted seal
Dusted o'er with golden meal.
Only there's a droning where
Yon bright beetle shines in air,
Tracks it in its gleaming flight
With a slanting beam of light,
Rising in the sunshine higher,
Till its shards flame out like fire.

Every other thing is still,
Save the ever-wakeful rill,
Whose cool murmur only throws
Cooler comfort round repose;
Or some ripple in the sea
Of leafy boughs, where, lazily,
Tired summer, in her bower
Turning with the noontide hour,
Heaves a slumbrous breath ere she
Once more slumbers peacefully.

O 'tis easeful here to lie
Hidden from noon's scorching eye,
In this grassy cool recess
Musing thus of quietness.

❧ *Country Veranda* ❧

JOHN TRANTER

I—DRY WEATHER

This country veranda's a box for storing the sky —
    slopes, acres of air
    bleached and adrift there.

From outside, a shade-filled stage, from inside
    a quiet cinema, empty
    but for the rustling view

where a parrot scribbles a crooked scrawl of crayon
    and off-stage a crow
    laments his loneliness

and six neat magpies, relaxed but quite soon
    off to a General Meeting
    stroll, chortle and yarn.

When the summer sun cracks the thermometer, laze
    there in a deck chair,
    shake out the paper

and relax with the local news: who won the cake
    in the Ambulance raffle;
    what the Council did

about the gravel concession down at the creek, who
    suffered a nasty fall
    but should be well in a week.

II—RAIN

From that open room where sheets hang out to dry—
    cool, wet pages
    whose verses evaporate—

you stare out at the trees semaphoring their sophistry:
    their tangled, pointless plots
    and obsessive paraphernalia,

drenched among the spacious palaces of vertical rain
    where no phone rings
    and neighbours are distant.

Behind that ridge of mist and blowing eucalypt tops
    the world waited once:
    exotic, inexhaustible.

You've been there now, and found that it's not much fun.
    On the veranda, silence
    fills the long afternoon.

Trisha Dixon (b.1953)
Glenara, Italianate House, Bulla, Victoria 1998
col. transparency; 6.0 x 6.0 cm
Pictures Collection, nla.pic-an23135065

❦ *The Forest* ❦

JUDITH WRIGHT

When first I knew this forest
its flowers were strange.
Their different forms and faces
changed with the seasons' change—

white violets smudged with purple,
the wild-ginger spray,
ground-orchids small and single
haunted my day;

the thick-fleshed Murray-lily,
flame-tree's bright blood,
and where the creek runs shallow,
the cunjevoi's green hood.

When first I knew this forest,
time was to spend,
and time's renewing harvest
could never reach an end.

Now that its vines and flowers
are named and known,
like long-fulfilled desires
those first strange joys are gone.

My search is further.
There's still to name and know
beyond the flowers I gather
that one that does not wither—
the truth from which they grow.

Trisha Dixon (b.1953)
Eucalypts at Kangaroo Ground, Melbourne, Victoria 1999
col. transparency; 6.0 x 6.0 cm
Private Collection

Trisha Dixon (b.1953)
Glenara, Bulla, Victoria 1998
col. slide; 35 mm
Pictures Collection, nla.pic-an23134944

❧ *June Morning* ❧

HUGH McCRAE

The twisted apple, with rain and magian fire
Caught in its branches from the early dawn,
I, from my bed, through the fogged pane see, and desire
Of its sharp sweetness, something: green the lawn
And stiff with pointed spears of daffodils run wild;
The sluggard sun draws the drowned Daphne back to life —
And all the drowsy doves, brown sparrows, husband, wife,
Are stirring on the housetops—child to early child
Coo-eeing and calling; blind windows open eyes …
And in the air the bitter fragrance floats
Of someone's gardener's pipe; I will arise
And in the stinging shower forget gold motes,
Thick pillows, blankets, books; travel the wholesome road
And give my body to the sun.

❧ Grown for Their Leaves ❧

JOAN LAW-SMITH

Why do I always plan for flowers
In autumn's cold or flush of spring
There's a simpler way to furnish air,
A leaf is such a lovely thing.

Trisha Dixon (b.1953)
Garden, Glen Rannoch, Mount Macedon, Victoria 1998
col. slide; 35 mm
Pictures Collection, nla.pic-an23098634

❧ Pranks of Nature ❧

JOAN LAW-SMITH

The silver birch tree's magic stem.
The gently spotted guinea hen;
The lady-bird — a come by chance,
The peacock's flaunting arrogance;
The fox-glove's pendant freckled face,
 Some orchids with their quaint grimace;
The green frog's metronomic croak,
The bee-lines on a violet's throat;
The brolga's captivating dance,
The sun-dew's strange carnivorous sense;
The toadstool's flushed anatomy,
The seed pods of a banksia tree;
This art of nature makes us smile,
If we have time to gaze awhile.

Trisha Dixon (b.1953)
Pine Grove, Cavendish, Victoria 1997
col. slide; 35 mm
Private Collection

Trisha Dixon (b.1953)
Narmbool, Elaine, Victoria 1998
col. transparency; 6.0 x 6.0 cm
Private Collection

❧ The Garden ❧

JAMES McAULEY

Afternoon light shines like blood
In the dark-red prunus tree,
Blackbirds stab the lawn for food,
Madame Hardy lures the bee,
Flagstone cracks are seamed with thyme;
Lateness is my fear, my crime.

Autumn settles; yet in me
Something burns and festers still,
Shrills the anger of the bee,
Daunts the blackbird's orange bill.
I can pray, but not atone:
Let this be the hour of None,

And this troubled murmur, breathed
On the resinous calm air
Where the flasks of summer seethed,
Be a grace against despair:
From the wounded tree a balm,
From the depths a kind of psalm.

Spring — The Awakening

BETTY CASEY LITCHFIELD

Pale violet lace
Tenderly kissing
A silvered grey wall.
Buds on the apple tree,
Pink, shell-tipped infants
Frightened to fall.

Transparent lilac,
Snow-drops newly born.
Fragile frilled daisies
Tip-toeing the lawn.

Slender birch trembling,
Bluebells underneath.
To herald this awakening
My all, I bequeath.

Trisha Dixon (b.1953)
Wild Garden at Bobundara, Cooma, New South Wales 1996
col. transparency; 6.0 x 6.0 cm
Private Collection

Trisha Dixon (b.1953)
Coolringdon, Cooma, New South Wales [between 1989 and 1992]
col. transparency; 6.0 x 6.0 cm
Pictures Collection, nla.pic-an10634434-11

❧ A Stream — Coolringdon ❧

BETTY CASEY LITCHFIELD

Oh, What a beautiful stream you are
With reeds and rocks and a falling star!
Silver ripples that splash and glide
Over stepping stones to the other side.

Why are the slender reeds golden tonight?
magical fingers, a lover's delight.
Is it a brown duck I see on the pool,
Or a wayward pixie ariding his stool?

Don't answer my questions,
Don't shatter my dreams,
let me live on believing it's all as it seems;
That some day in passing I'll stand here again
Wrapped in love and in laughter
A life without pain.

❧ *Pieces!* ❧

BETTY CASEY LITCHFIELD

Please don't sweep the crimson
leaves from the terrace,
Leave them undisturbed and beautiful
Just as they are now.
Don't sweep away the golden leaves
from beneath the poplar,
Leave them scattered all over the lawns,
Each one magnificent, bewildering;
Each one a fragment of an earth-born star.

Trisha Dixon (b.1953)
House and Garden, Durrol, Mount Macedon, Victoria 1999
col. transparency; 6.0 x 6.0 cm
Pictures Collection, nla.pic-an23123752

Trisha Dixon (b.1953)
Hascombe Garden, Ponds, Mount Macedon, Victoria 1997
col. slide; 35 mm
Pictures Collection, nla.pic-an23122240

Acknowledgments

'Australian Autumn' from *My Country: Australian Poetry and Short Stories: Two Hundred Years. Volume 1: Beginnings—1930s*, selected and introduced by Leonie Kramer, Sydney: Lansdown Press, 1985. Courtesy of New Holland Publishers.

'Dear Little Cottage' from *Collected Poems: John Shaw Neilson 1872—1942*, a digital text sponsored by the Australian Literature Electronic Gateway, University of Sydney Library, 2000. First published as *Collected Poems*, John Shaw Neilson, Melbourne: Lothian Book Publishing, 1934.

'Amongst the Roses' from *Poems and Songs by Henry Kendall*, Sydney: J.R. Clarke, 1862.

'Songs of Murray's Brigade' from *Complete Poems* by Banjo Paterson, Sydney: Harper Collins (Angus and Robertson Classics), 2001. Courtesy of Harper Collins Publishers.

'Autumn Rain' from *Bone Scan* by Gwen Harwood, Sydney: Angus and Robertson, 1988. Courtesy of Penguin Australia.

'Florobiography' from *Whirling* by Chris Wallace-Crabbe, Oxford: Oxford University Press, 1998. Courtesy of Carcanet Press Limited.

'Flowering Eucalypt in Autumn' from *The People's Otherworld* by Les A. Murray, Sydney: Angus and Robertson, 1983. Courtesy of Margaret Connolly.

'The Lark' from *An Austral Garden: An Anthology of Australian Verse*, ed. M. P. Hansen and D. McLachlan, Melbourne: George Roberston and Co., 1929. Courtesy of Joan Margaret Allen.

'Morning Peace' from *An Austral Garden: An Anthology of Australian Verse*, ed. M. P. Hansen and D. McLachlan, Melbourne: George Robertson and Co., 1929.

'Grown for Their Leaves' from *The Uncommon Garden* by Joan Law-Smith, Melbourne: Women's Committee of the National Trust of Australia, 1983. Courtesy of Ann Wyld.

'Country Veranda' from *Australian Poetry in the Twentieth Century*, ed. Robert Gray and Geoffrey Lehmann, Melbourne: William Heinemann Australia, 1991. Courtesy of John Tranter.

'A Mid-Summer Noon in the Australian Forest' from *Poems* by Charles Harpur, Melbourne: George Robertson, 1883.

'The Forest' *A Human Pattern: Selected Poems by Judith Wright*, Sydney: ETT Imprint, 1996. Courtesy of ETT Imprint.

'June Morning' from *From the Ballads to Brennan: Poetry in Australia Volume 1*, chosen by T. Inglis Moore, Sydney: Angus and Robertson, 1964. Courtesy of ETT Imprint.

'Déjeuner sur l'herbe' from *Penguin Book of Modern Australian Poetry*, ed. John Tranter and Philip Mead, Melbourne: Penguin Australia, 1991. Courtesy of University of Queensland Press.

'Pranks of Nature' from *The Uncommon Garden* by Joan Law-Smith, [Melbourne:] Women's Committee of the National Trust of Australia (Victoria), 1983. Courtesy of Ann Wyld.

'The Garden' from *James McAuley Collected Poems 1936–1970*, Sydney: Angus and Robertson, 1971. Courtesy of Harper Collins Publishers.

'Spring—The Awakening' from *Mountain Snow, Monaro Shadows* by Betty Casey Litchfield, Cooma, NSW: Cootapatamba Publications, 1984. Courtesy of Coolringdon Pastoral Co.

'A Stream—Coolringdon' from *Coolringdon Garden* by Trisha Dixon, Canberra: Australian Garden History Society, ACT Monaro and Riverina Group, 1998. Courtesy of Coolringdon Pastoral Co.

'Pieces!' from *Mountain Snow, Monaro Shadows* by Betty Casey Litchfield, Cooma, NSW: Cootapatamba Publications, 1984. Courtesy of Coolringdon Pastoral Co.

The National Library of Australia wishes to thank Trisha Dixon for giving permission to reproduce her photographs throughout this book.